IN FOCUS

REPTILES

KINGFISHER
LONDON & NEW YORK

Copyright © Macmillan Publishers International Ltd 2017
Published in the United States by Kingfisher,
175 Fifth Ave., New York, NY 10010
Kingfisher is an imprint of Macmillan Children's Books, London

Distributed in the U.S. and Canada by Macmillan,
175 Fifth Ave., New York, NY 10010

Library of Congress Cataloging-in-Publication data has been applied for.

Series editor: Hayley Down
Designer: Jeni Child

ISBN 978-0-7534-7367-2 (HB)
ISBN 978-0-7534-7375-7 (PB)

Kingfisher books are available for special promotions
and premiums. For details contact: Special Markets
Department, Macmillan, 175 Fifth Ave.,
New York, NY 10010.

For more information, please visit
www.kingfisherbooks.com

Printed in China

9 8 7 6 5 4 3 2 1

1TR/0916/WKT/UG/128GSM

Picture credits
The Publisher would like to thank the following for permission to reproduce their material.
Top = t; Bottom = b; Middle = m; Left = l; Right = r
Front cover: Alamy/Chris Mattison; Back cover: iStock/Snowleopard1; Back cover flap: iStock/KongSan; Pages: 1 Shutterstock/
Voloymyr Burdiak; 3 iStock/Paulina Lenting-Smulder; 4_5 iStock/Isaac 74; 4t Shutterstock/Janelle Lugge; 4m iStock/Csondy; 4b
iStock/Stuartb;5 iStock/Serge_Vero; 6 iStock/Sami Sert; 7t iStock/chrispecoraro; 7m Getty/Joe McDonald; 7b Alamy/blickwinkel/
Hartl; 8–9 Shutterstock/Janelle Lugge; 10–11 iStock/BrianEKushner; 11 iStock/Mark Kostich; 12tl iStock/kjorgen; 12tr iStock/amwu;
12bl iStock/Snowleopard1; 12br iStock/triggerfishsaul; 13bl iStock/CJ_Romas; 13br Alam/Tim Cuff; 14–15 Alamy Alexey Senin; 16m
iStock/ LukeWaitPhotography; 17t Alamy/Mike Parry/Minden Pictures; 17b iStock/AlbertoLoyo; 18–19 Getty/ Martin Harvey; 20–21
iStock/walkingmoon; 20 Shutterstock/Ahturner; 22t iStock/NNehring; 22bl Alamy Ben Nottidge; 22br iStock/andipantz; 23t iStock/
estivillml; 23bl Getty/Bob Elsdale; 23br Alamy/Heather Angel; 24–25 Shutterstock/Rusty Dodson; 26 iStock/triggerfishsaul; 27t
iStock/italiansight; 27m Shutterstock/FamVeld; 27b Alamy/Jurgen Freund; 28 Shutterstock/Mavadee; 29t Shutterstock/JI de Wet; 29b
Nature PL/Anup Shah; 30–31 Getty/Jenny Rainbow/EyeEm; 32(1) Alamy/Martin Harvey; 32 (2) iStock/markhiggins; 33 (3) Shutterstock/
TomTietz; 33 (4) iStock/wcpmedia; 33 (5) Alamy/Tobias Bernhard Raff; 33 (6) iStock/wrangle; 33 (7) Alamy/Blickwinkel/Layer; 33 (8)
Alamy/ Junior Bildarchiv GmbH; 33 (9) Alamy/Martin Harvey; 33 (10) iStock/ DarshanTuppad; 34 iStock/Stuartb; 35t Getty/Auscape;
35m Alamy/David Kleyn; 35b Shutterstock/Edwin Butter; 36–37 FLPA/Tom and Peter Gardner; 36 iStock/ppl58; 38–39 Alamy/
Don Johnston_IH; 40–41 Getty/Bence Mate/Nature Picture Library; 42t iStock/Snowleopard1; 42bl iStock001_Quadrixx; 42br iStock/
michaelgatewood; 43tl iStock/edevansuk43tr iStock/petesphotography; 43bl Alamy/Stephen Dalton/Minden Pictures; 43br iStock/
LPETTET; 44 Shutterstock/Rich Carey; 45t iStock/Serge_Vero; 45b Alamy/Getty/Bence Mate/ Nature Picture Library; 46 iStock/
ian35mm; 47t Alamy/John Warburton-Lee Photography; 47m iStock/Snowleopard1; 47b Alamy/blickwinkel/Teigler; 48 (1) iStock/
USO; 49 (2) iStock/LPETTET; 49 (3) iStock/unclegene; 49 (4) Alamy/Jason Ondreicka; 49 (5) Shutterstock/Ashley Whitworth; 49
(6) Gety/Simon Marloe/EyeEm; 49 (7) iStock/Mark kOSTICH; 49 (8) Shutterstock/MirasWonderland; 49 (9) iStock/StuPorts; 49 (10)
Shutterstock/NickEvansKZN; 50 iStock/SnowLeopard1; 51t Shutterstock/Stuart G Porter; 51m Shutterstock/Oksana Golubeva; 51b
iStock/mspoli; 52–53 iStock/Gwengoat; 53 Getty/Jerry Young; 54 FLPA/Frans Lanting; 5t Shutterstock/Zdenek Rosenthaler; 55b
iStock/wrangle; 56–57 Getty/Mint Images – Frans Lanting; 58 (1) iStock/blende10; 59 (2) Alamy/Diana Meister; 59 (3) Shutterstock/
Matt Cornish; 59 (4) iStock/Laures; 59 (5) iStock/kevdog818; 59 (6) Alamy/Joe Blossom; 59 (7) Alamy/Daniel Heuclin/Nature Picture
Library; 59 (8) Shutterstock/Matt Jeppson; 59 (9) Getty Mint Images- Frans Lanting; 59 (10) iStock/EcoPic; 60 Shutterstock/febriyanto
reinaldy; 61 iStock/Mark Kastich; 62 iStock/wrangle; 63 Shutterstock/M Reza Saptodi.

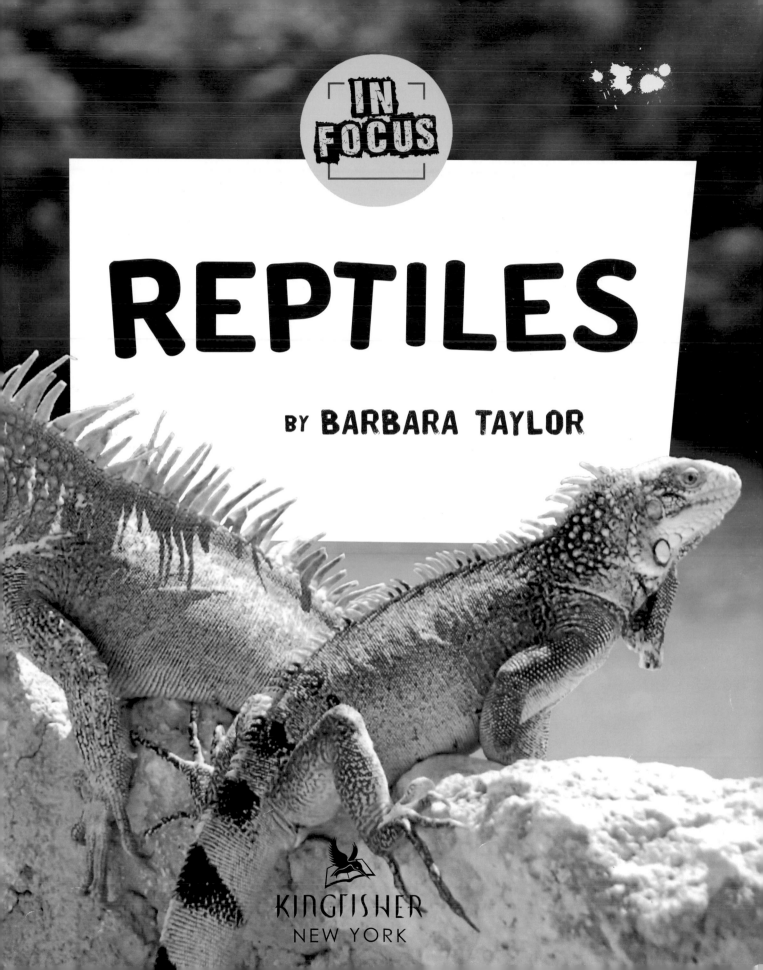

IN FOCUS

REPTILES

BY **BARBARA TAYLOR**

KINGFISHER
NEW YORK

CONTENTS

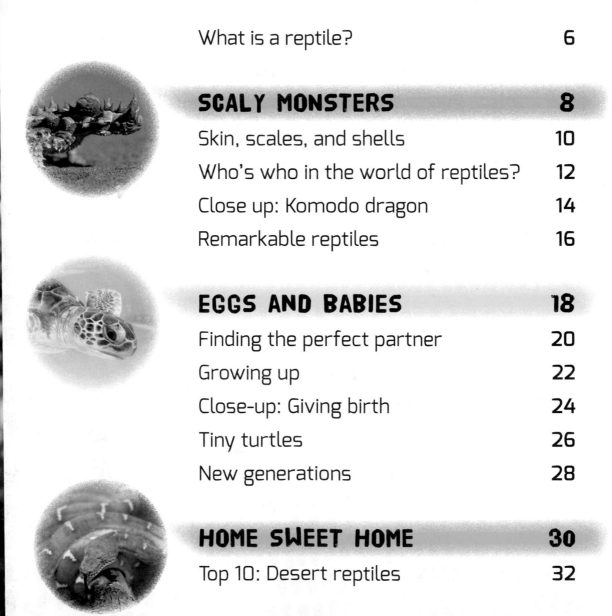

SCALY SURVIVORS   40

WHAT IS A REPTILE?

Reptiles are animals with scaly skin, such as lizards and crocodiles. They have a bony internal **skeleton** to support and protect their body. Unlike birds and mammals, reptiles rely on their surroundings to warm up and cool down—they are **cold-blooded**. Most reptiles live in warm places and lay eggs with shells, but some reptiles give birth to live young. Reptiles have lived on Earth for millions of years, and the most famous reptiles of all—the **dinosaurs**—once dominated our planet. These monsters died out long ago, but more than 8,000 **species** of reptile share our world today.

Chinese water dragon

INSIDE YOU'LL FIND ...

... sun worshippers

Reptiles love **SUNBATHING!** They absorb warmth in order to have enough energy to survive. Birds and mammals keep warm by burning food to release energy. Reptiles do not need to eat to keep warm, so they can go longer without a meal.

... scaly creatures

SCALES are mostly made of keratin. This is the substance that your hair and fingernails are made of, as well as the claws, hooves, and feathers of other animals. Scales keep reptiles dry and seal moisture inside their body.

... life cycles

Most reptile **EGGS,** such as snake eggs, have soft, leathery shells, which are different from hard bird eggs. Some reptiles however, such as tortoises, crocodiles, and geckos, lay eggs with hard shells.

SCALY MONSTERS

SKIN, SCALES, AND SHELLS

How do reptiles use their scales? Your questions about the scaly skin of reptiles answered.

Diamondback terrapin turtle

Which lizards look like dinosaurs?

Many lizards have spines or crests, which make them look like dinosaurs, such as Stegosaurus! A lizard's spines or crests are made of rough, **granular** scales that rise into spiky points. They provide a good form of defense and sometimes help to attract a mate.

Which reptiles have giant scales?

Turtles and tortoises have giant scales, called **scutes**, that cover their bony shell. Their shell acts like body armor to protect the turtle or tortoise from **predators**! Land tortoises have high, domed, or knobbly shells. Water-dwelling turtles have a flatter, more **streamlined** shell to help them swim.

How do snakes change their clothes?

A snake can wriggle out of its old skin. The skin comes off in one piece, similar to a person peeling off a sock. Underneath is a new set of scales. Replacing an old skin in this way is called **sloughing** (say "sluffing"). It allows the snake to grow bigger and replaces damaged or worn-out scales.

Which lizard is like an underground train?

Slow worms are lizards with small, smooth, rounded scales. These help the slow worm to burrow underground because its smooth skin slides through the soil easily. Slow worms have no legs—these would catch against the sides of their burrow and slow the slow worm down.

marine iguanas

coahuilan box turtle

LIZARDS AND SNAKES

More than half of all reptiles are lizards, with more than 5,000 different species. Snakes make up the second-largest group, with more than 3,000 species. Snakes have no legs, while most lizards have four legs to run fast, as well as a long tail. All snakes and most lizards are meat-eaters, but a few lizards feed on plants. The marine iguana even eats seaweed!

TURTLES AND TORTOISES

The only reptiles with a bony shell are turtles and tortoises. There are about 300 different species, which have lived on our planet since the days of the dinosaurs. Turtles and tortoises have sharp, horny jaws, but no teeth. Some eat plants and some eat meat, but many are **omnivores**, which means they eat all types of food.

green tree python

green sea turtle

12

WHO IN THE WORLD OF REPTILES?

There are four main groups of reptiles alive today. They are: lizards and snakes, turtles and tortoises, the crocodile family, and a group with just one species—the tuatara.

CROCODILE FAMILY

Fierce hunters, the 23 species in the crocodile family make up one of the smallest reptile groups. They lurk in rivers, lakes, swamps, or the ocean, waiting to snap up **prey** with their huge jaws and sharp teeth. This family includes alligators, caimans, and gharials. Ancient relatives of the crocodile family lived with the dinosaurs nearly 200 million years ago.

TERRIFIC TUATARA

The rare tuatara is a unique reptile that lives only on a few islands off the coast of New Zealand. It was named after the crest on its back—its name means "spiny back." Tuataras live in burrows and come out at night to ambush prey, such as insects, slugs, and worms. They have hardly changed over millions of years and look very similar to their dinosaur relatives.

gharial

tuatara

KOMODO DRAGON

Did you know that there are real dragons? The Komodo dragon is just as incredible as the dragons of myths and legends. Even its long, forked tongue reminds people of fire-breathing dragons! This fierce reptile is the only lizard known to attack people. If prey manages to escape from the dragon's sharp claws and jagged teeth, deadly **bacteria** in its bite make sure that the victim dies soon afterward.

More about Komodo dragons:

Size: males up to 10 ft. (3 m long)
Average lifespan: 30 years or more
Food: almost any kind of meat, from water buffalo and deer to wild boar and small lizards
Weird fact: Young dragons often roll in poop to stop bigger dragons from eating them!

REMARKABLE REPTILES

Discover incredible facts about extraordinary reptiles.

TUATARAS have a third eye on top of their head. It's not used for seeing things, but may sense sunlight.

The **BIG-HEADED TURTLE** has such a big head that it can't pull its head back inside its shell for safety. Instead, its protruding head has a bony roof for protection.

A big **SNAKE** may have up to 400 bones in its long **backbone**, with hundreds of ribs joined to it.

The longest snake in the world is the **RETICULATED PYTHON**, which can reach lengths of nearly 30 ft. (9 m). That's as long as a bus! This snake is big enough to tackle deer and pigs for lunch.

A monster called **MEDUSA** from an ancient Greek myth had writhing snakes for her hair. One look from Medusa turned people to stone.

Some **SEA TURTLES** have a very unusual diet. Leatherbacks eat mainly jellyfish, while a hawksbill turtle's favorite food is sponges!

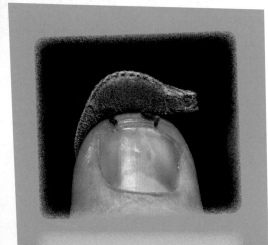

The world's smallest reptile is smaller than a human fingernail! It's a teeny, tiny **LEAF CHAMELEON**, which is a type of lizard.

A large **SALTWATER CROCODILE** weighs as much as three cars! It is the heaviest living reptile in the world.

Some reptiles live for a very long time. **GIANT TORTOISES** may live more than 200 years, and some crocodiles and tuataras live for 100 years.

EGGS AND BABIES

FINDING THE PERFECT PARTNER

Your questions about reptiles' courtship displays answered.

anole lizard

Why do male snakes wrestle each other?

Rival male snakes, such as adders, sometimes compete in a test of strength, like people in a wrestling match. They rear up, twist their necks together, and try to push each other to the ground. The strongest male wins the chance to mate with a female, while the loser gives up and crawls away in defeat. The snakes don't usually hurt each other when they wrestle.

Which lizards fly the flag?

Male anole lizards show off the colored "flag," or throat flap, under their chin to attract females or warn off rivals. If two males are the same size, they may "fly the flag" at each other for hours at a time. A smaller male will give in to a larger male very quickly.

Which turtles have super-sized claws?

Some male turtles, such as painted turtles, have three extra-long claws on their front feet. During **courtship**, the male chases the female through the water and strokes her face with his long claws. If the female wants to mate, she strokes the male's legs with her own claws.

Why are male alligators so noisy?

To attract a mate, male alligators open their mouth wide and bellow loudly. Their throaty roar carries long distances, telling females where to find them and warning rival males: "Stay away or I will fight you!" When one male starts to bellow, the others join in!

GROWING UP

Most reptiles hatch out of eggs, but a few reptiles give birth to fully developed young. Baby reptiles look like miniature versions of their parents and are usually left to live alone.

LIZARDS AND SNAKES

Most lizards and snakes lay eggs with soft, leathery shells. A few lizards and snakes guard their eggs. When the babies are ready to hatch, they use a sharp "egg tooth" on their snout (nose) to break free of the shell. Some lizards and snakes give birth to live young, which have grown inside their mother's body.

juvenile Australian carpet pythons

TURTLES AND TORTOISES

All turtles and tortoises lay eggs on land, so their babies can breathe **oxygen** from the air. Tortoises and some turtles lay hard-shelled eggs, but the eggs of sea turtles and some river turtles have soft shells. The number of eggs laid varies from just one to more than a hundred! Mothers do not usually care for their eggs or babies.

leatherback turtles

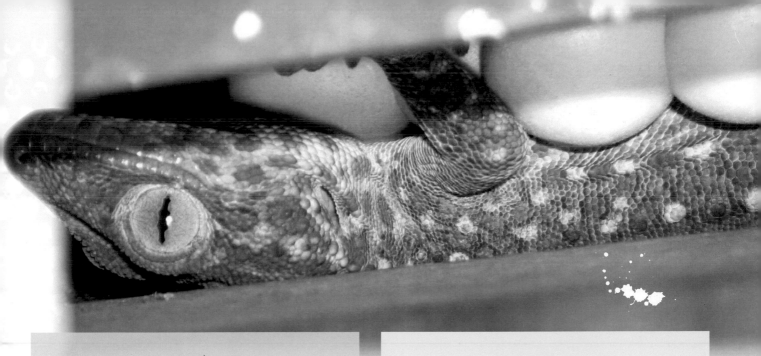

CROCODILE FAMILY

Females in the crocodile family all lay eggs with hard shells. They lay from about 10 to 90 eggs at a time. Alligators, caimans, and some crocodiles build nests out of plants and soil. Other crocodiles and gharials dig holes for their eggs. These mothers are the only reptiles to both guard their eggs and protect their **hatchlings**.

TERRIFIC TUATARAS

Every two to five years, a female tuatara lays up to 19 eggs in a nesting burrow. The baby tuataras take about a year to hatch. Higher temperatures in the nest produce more male tuataras and lower temperatures produce more females. Mother tuataras do not protect their eggs or babies.

crocodile

tuatara

CLOSE UP

GIVING BIRTH

Snakes that give birth to live young include boas, rattlesnakes, garter snakes, adders, and most sea snakes. The babies develop inside the mother's body, where they are warm and protected. They are surrounded by see-through bags, called membranes (instead of shells), and usually get their food from a yolk sac. The mother snake gives birth to 6–50 babies at a time, after a labor that may last for hours.

More about garter snakes:

Food: slugs, worms, lizards, amphibians, minnows, and rodents

Weird fact: Garter snakes hibernate (rest) through the winter in large groups. They mate when they emerge from hibernation.

red-sided garter snake

TINY TURTLES

The life of a green sea turtle starts as a small egg—the size of a ping-pong ball—buried on a sandy beach in a warm, tropical place. The female returns to the beach where she hatched out of an egg herself. She drags herself slowly up the beach in the cool night air and uses her flippers to dig a nesting hole. She lays about 120 eggs in the hole, then covers the eggs with sand and returns to the sea, leaving the eggs (and baby turtles) to fend for themselves.

Female green sea turtles lay several **clutches** of eggs a year but only nest every two or four years. They start laying eggs when they are between 25 and 50 years old, making long journeys from their feeding areas to their nesting sites. Some female green sea turtles swim as far as 1,300 mi. (2,000 km) to lay their eggs.

green sea turtle

hatchling
breaks free

About two months after the eggs are laid, the baby turtles **HATCH**. They work together to dig their way out of the nest. This is very hard work, and it may take them up to three days to struggle free.

The **BABY** turtles race toward the sea, trying to dodge predators, such as birds, crabs, and racoons, to avoid being eaten. A few lucky hatchlings make it as far as the water, where they dive into the waves.

hatchlings
on the beach

hatchling
in the sea

Tiny turtles **SWIM** nonstop until they reach deeper water, where they are at less risk from predators. They live in floating mats of seaweed in the open ocean until they are big enough to survive in feeding areas near the shore.

Some female reptiles, such as **GECKOS**, can produce young without males. This helps them survive in places where there are no males to mate with.

NEW GENERATIONS

Reptiles use different methods to produce new generations and continue the species.

The eggs of the **AFRICAN LEOPARD TORTOISE** take over a year to hatch.

- The smallest number of eggs laid in one clutch by sea turtles is about 50. **FLATBACK TURTLES** lay this many eggs at a time. Hawksbill turtles, however, may lay over 200 eggs in one clutch!

- **GRASS SNAKES** lay their eggs in piles of rotting plants. The heat given off by decomposing (rotting) plants speeds up the development of the eggs.

- **FEMALE PYTHONS** coil around their eggs to protect them from predators. The female Indian python twitches her muscles to warm up her body so the heat will help her young develop.

- The eggs of the **SALTWATER CROCODILE** are up to twice the size of a chicken's eggs. It takes a female "saltie" about 15 minutes to lay between 20 and 90 eggs in her nest.

A mother **NILE CROCODILE** carries up to 15 hatchlings in her mouth and takes them safely to the water.

TOP 10 DESERT REPTILES

How do reptiles survive in really hot places with very little food and water?

1 Sidewinders

Many desert snakes are called "sidewinders" because they fling themselves sideways across the sand to keep their body off the hot sand as much as possible.

2 Thorny devil

The Australian thorny devil survives in dry places by drinking the dew that **condenses** on its body at night.

7 Spiny-tailed agama lizard

The spiny-tailed agama lizard survives in dry places by using the fat stored in its chubby tail!

3 Desert tortoise

Desert tortoises may catch rainwater on their shell or dig holes to collect rare rainfall. Some can survive a year without water!

8 Web-footed gecko

This gecko has long legs to keep its body off the hot sand. It also hops to let its feet cool down.

4 Nile crocodile

Rare Nile crocodiles, living on the edge of the Sahara desert, spend dry seasons sleeping. They don't eat and hardly move at all, which helps them survive harsh, dry times.

9 Horned viper

The scaly horns of the desert horned viper work like sunglasses to shade its eyes. It shuffles under the sand to hide from the heat and wait for prey.

5 Sand lizard

Sand lizards "swim" through the sand, like a fish swims through water. They spend a lot of time underground to escape the heat of the sun.

10 Sand boa

This snake spends most of its time buried in the sand with just its head sticking out, waiting for passing prey to pounce on!

6 Pancake tortoise

The shell of the pancake tortoise is so flat that it can squeeze under rocks to avoid the hot sun.

Which desert reptile is your number one?

RAIN FOREST REPTILES

Reptiles lurk everywhere in **rain forests**. The weather here is warm all year round, so reptiles can stay active all the time. There are plenty of places for them to live, from the tree trunks and branches to the forest floor and rain forest rivers. There is also plenty of food for reptiles in rain forests.

They eat insects, birds, bats, rats, and frogs, as well as other reptiles. Many rain forest reptiles are well **camouflaged** to hide from danger. Tree-living reptiles are good climbers. They have sharp claws, grippy pads on their feet, or a long, curly tail, which they use to cling tightly to branches.

tree boa coiled
around branch

common flying dragon

FLYING LIZARDS spread out their skin to form "wings" that catch the air, helping them glide from tree to tree. Flying snakes suck in their stomach to create a C-shaped body, rather like a parachute, and float down slowly from branch to branch.

parrot snake

To grip tree branches, a **TREE SNAKE** uses ridges on its belly scales and a special prehensile (gripping) tail to coil around branches. It holds on tightly and shoots out its head to grab prey with its sharp teeth.

caiman

Rain forest streams and swamps are home to **DWARF CAIMANS** and African dwarf crocodiles. Here they avoid competition with larger caimans and crocodiles.

RIVER AND SWAMP DWELLERS

Which reptiles lurk in the water? Your questions answered.

Which lizard is good at diving?

Green iguanas like to sunbathe on tree branches around mangrove swamps. If they feel threatened, they may leap 30 ft. (10 m) or more into the water below. They swim to the bottom of the water and hide there for up to half an hour.

snake-necked turtle

Which water snake is a mammoth meat-eater?

The heaviest snake in the world, the anaconda, lives in the rivers of the Amazon rain forest. Anacondas weigh up to 500 lbs. (227 kg)—that's more than five times heavier than a child! They catch large prey, such as caimans, deer, and even jaguars, which provide enough energy for them to survive for a long time.

Which reptile uses a snorkel?

The snake-necked turtle has a very long neck and a tube nose that works like a snorkel. The turtle lurks underwater and pushes its snorkel nose up above the surface of the water to take a breath of air.

When does a floating log suddenly come to life?

Alligators float quietly in the swamps of southeastern USA. Their dark colors, rough, barklike scales, and the tiny water plants that decorate their back make them look just like floating logs. But if a prey animal comes within reach, the alligators suddenly come to life, and their giant jaws open and snap shut with surprising speed!

SEA MONSTER

The marine iguana of the Galapagos Islands is the only lizard that swims and feeds in the sea. It uses its powerful tail to swim strongly and feeds on seaweed. Large males dive as deep as 32 ft. (10 m) in search of a seaweed banquet. When they are not swimming in the sea, marine iguanas bask in the sun so their body is warm enough to digest their food.

More about marine iguanas:

Average size of adults: 2 2.5 ft.
(0.6–0.75 metres)
Food: seaweed
Average lifespan: 5-12 years
Weird fact: As their diet contains a lot of salt, these iguanas sneeze out a salty spray from their nostrils from time to time. This often lands on their head, making them look as if they have white hair.

SCALY SURVIVORS

MOVERS AND

From speedy lizards and fast-swimming turtles to slithering snakes and plodding tortoises, reptiles have adapted well to moving through different environments.

SWING AND SLIDE

Even though they have no legs, snakes can glide over the ground, swim through water, and even climb trees. Snakes are not fast movers—a person can walk faster than most snakes! Snakes have a flexible body, which they swing from side to side in S-shaped curves. They can also move in a straight line by using their belly scales to grip the ground.

dice snake

TAIL POWER

Members of the crocodile family glide through the water with slow, S-shaped sweeps of their powerful tail. They hold their legs close to their body to make it more streamlined, sometimes using their legs like **rudders** to change direction. On land, these reptiles move in a high walk, with their short legs under the body and their tail off the ground.

Nile crocodile

SHAKERS

AGILE ACROBATS

Lizards are the fastest reptiles on the planet. Most lizards have four legs, which stick out from the side of their body. This means their body moves in S-shaped curves. Some lizards run very fast on all fours, while others run on just two legs, with the front of their body held up in the air. Some tree lizards may have a special prehensile tail and toes with extra-sharp claws.

common flying dragon

PLODDERS AND SWIMMERS

On land, a tortoise's heavy shell makes fast movement impossible. Instead, it plods along slowly and carefully on its strong legs. In contrast, its turtle relatives in the water swim quickly, using powerful flippers and webbed feet to help them glide gracefully through the water. Sea and river turtles have a lighter, more streamlined shell to make swimming easier.

desert tortoise

LEGS, TOES, AND TAILS

Rowing, swimming, weightlifting, galloping, and tobogganing ... some reptiles would definitely win medals if they entered the Olympics!

Some **SEA TURTLES** swim as fast as 18.5 mi. (30 km) per hour, which is three times faster than the fastest human swimmers, such as Olympic champion Michael Phelps!

CROCODILES sometimes move fast by sliding across muddy ground on their belly—a bit like a living toboggan. They use their legs to push themselves along.

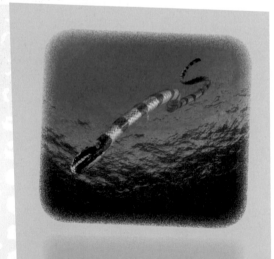

SEA SNAKES have a flat tail, like an oar, which gives them extra power to push through the water.

FRINGE-TOED LIZARDS have a series of special scales on their toes, which help them to move across soft, sliding desert sands without sinking in.

GECKOS, such as the tokay gecko, have microscopic, hairlike hooks under their toe pads. This helps them cling to almost any surface and even walk upside down on ceilings!

The **PIG-NOSED TURTLE** is the only freshwater turtle with flippers. It "flies" underwater, moving both its front and back flippers at the same time. Sea turtles use only their front flippers for swimming and their back flippers as rudders and brakes.

GIANT TORTOISES have legs like elephants' legs—sturdy columns to support their massive weight. They weigh over 900 lbs. (417 kg) so a person could not lift them!

The **BASILISK LIZARD** runs across the surface of the water at up to 5 mi. (8.4 km) per hour. Young basilisks can keep running for 6–12 mi. (10–20 m)!

SURPRISING SENSES

Most reptiles pick up information from their surroundings through their senses of sight, smell, taste, and touch, but the sense of hearing is less important in snakes, tortoises, and turtles. Some reptiles have surprising ways of sensing their surroundings. Snakes and some lizards have a forked tongue that can taste and smell the air. Snakes have no outside ears or **eardrums**; instead they collect sound through an earbone joined to their jaw.

SCALY FACT

CROCODILES have more powerful senses than other reptiles. They have good eyesight and can see in color. Their pupils open wide to let in as much light as possible, and a special layer at the back of the eye reflects light, making their eyes glow in the dark.

monitor lizard

MONITOR LIZARDS flick their forked tongue in and out to collect scent particles from the air. The particles are analyzed in the roof of the mouth, helping the lizard to find food, meet a mate, or detect enemies.

tree boa

Some **SNAKES**, such as pit vipers, boas, or pythons, can detect the heat given off by warm-blooded animal prey, such as rats or birds. These snakes have "heat holes" in their face, which are sensitive to warmth. This helps them to hunt in the dark.

gibba turtle

Many **FRESHWATER TURTLES** have a finger of skin, called a barbel, hanging under their chin. This sensory structure may help them to find prey or a mate.

TOP 10 DANGEROUS BEASTS

Come face-to-face with our top ten super scary reptiles!

Death roll

The Nile crocodile is so big it can kill prey as large as wildebeest. Its jaws snap shut with tons of crushing pressure. To kill a wildebeest, a crocodile bites hard, drags it into deep water and rolls over until the wildebeest drowns.

2 Don't bite me!

The common snapping turtle can bite off your fingers! The jaws of this had-tempered predator snap shut with a crunch.

7 Dinosaur lookalikes

Some chameleons have horns for fighting, making them look like mini versions of the dinosaur Triceratops.

3 Gator attack

An alligator puffs up its body with air and hisses loudly to scare predators away.

8 Scorpion killer

The agama lizard crushes scorpions in its powerful jaws before the scorpion can use its sting.

4 Beastly bite

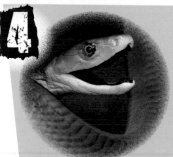

Mambas are very poisonous snakes, and a bite from one of these dangerous beasts can kill a person in just 10 minutes!

9 Brave beast

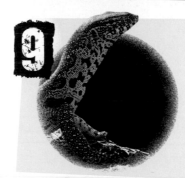

Nile monitor lizards are not afraid of snakes. They often crush snakes to death between their sharp teeth.

5 Beware, poison!

The bearded lizard is one of only two poisonous lizards in the world. Its bite is for defense—ouch!

10 Deadly stamp

Some wood turtles stomp on the ground to sound like rain. This trick lures worms straight into the turtle's waiting jaws.

6 Wrestling lizards

Monitor lizards are fierce wrestlers. They use their tail as a whip to defeat their opponents.

Which dangerous beast is your number one?

VENOMOUS SNAKES

folded fangs

SCALY FACT

VENOMOUS SNAKES inject venom through fangs. A viper (pictured) can fold back its fangs, while cobras, mambas, coral snakes, and sea kraits have fixed fangs. When venomous snakes bite, venom flows down grooves in their fangs and into the victim.

Did you know that fewer than a quarter of all snakes are venomous, or that **venom** of these snakes is a form of **saliva**?

spitting cobra

COBRA venom stops its victim's heart and lungs from working. The king cobra's venom is strong enough to kill an elephant! Spitting cobras squirt venom from their fangs. They aim for the eyes, where the venom causes terrible pain and sometimes blindness.

Belcher's sea snake

Many **SEA SNAKES** are highly poisonous. They eat mainly fish, which they swallow whole. Sea snakes paralyze and kill their prey quickly to stop the fish from escaping and to avoid being injured by a struggling fish inside their stomach!

warning stripes

There are more than 90 species of poisonous **CORAL SNAKES**. Their stripes send a signal to predators to keep away— and predators soon learn to leave these snakes alone!

FOOD
AND FEEDING

How do reptiles capture a meal? Your questions answered.

Which reptile feeds like a vacuum cleaner?

The matamata turtle lives at the bottom of muddy rivers in South America, waiting for fish to swim by. When it suddenly opens its big mouth and expands its huge throat, fish are sucked inside at lightning speed—too fast for the human eye to see!

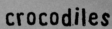

crocodiles

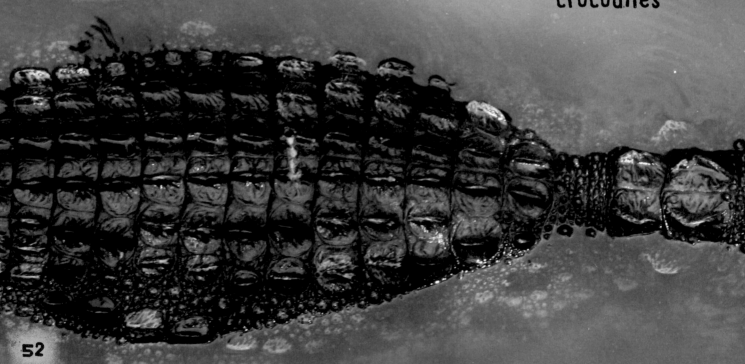

Which reptiles give the biggest hugs?

Some snakes, such as boas and pythons, kill their prey by giving it a gigantic hug! They coil their strong body around the prey, tightening their grip every time it breathes out. Eventually their victim can no longer breathe and dies from suffocation or shock. It often takes several days for one of these snakes to digest a big meal, but then they can go for weeks without eating.

Which reptiles like eggs for breakfast?

Eggs are the favorite food of egg-eating snakes because the eggs do not fight back! These snakes swallow the egg whole. Then they use the pointed ends of bones in their backbone to crack the eggshell. Finally, they swallow the contents of the egg and cough up the crushed shell.

Which reptiles are lazy hunters?

Most crocodiles lurk under the water, waiting for food to come to them. This saves a lot of energy. A crocodile's eyes and nostrils are on top of its head, which means it can breathe and look for prey while staying hidden from view. It lunges at its prey, trapping the animal with its strong jaws.

CUNNING COLORS

Some reptiles use their colors to hide, while others wear bright colors to stand out from the crowd.

The **BLUE-TONGUED SKINK** has a deep-blue tongue that it flicks in and out to startle and confuse predators.

Green is a camouflaging color for tree-living reptiles, such as **TREE SKINKS** or **TREE SNAKES**, which are almost invisible among the green leaves.

The brown colors and patterns of the **GABOON VIPER** make it disappear among the dead leaves of the forest floor as it lies in wait for rats, frogs, and birds to ambush.

HORNED LIZARDS match the sandy desert background, keeping them well hidden from predators such as hawks and snakes.

A **THORNY DEVIL** changes color to match its background. It also moves with jerky strides so it looks like a dry leaf blowing in the wind.

The Sri Lankan **KANGAROO LIZARD** has leaflike patterns on its head and body, and legs that look like thin twigs. When it hops into the dead leaves on the forest floor, it vanishes!

The **MILK SNAKE** is not poisonous, but it has similar colors and patterns to the poisonous coral snake. This clever trick fools predators into leaving it alone.

MATAMATA TURTLES move so slowly that plants grow on their shell. They blend in with the riverbed, so fish don't see them until they attack!

MASTERS OF DISGUISE

Many chameleons change color with the light, the temperature, or their mood. They can change color quite quickly by moving patches of color in their skin. Their camouflage colors help them to hide from predators and slowly sneak up on their insect prey. When a chameleon is close enough to an insect meal, it shoots out its long tongue at lightning speed (up to 19 ft./6 m per second), catching the insect on the sticky tip of its tongue.

More about chameleons:

Food: insects, birds, lizards
Size: from 0.5 in. (15 mm) to 27 in. (69 cm)
Average lifespan: 2–10 years
Weird fact: A chameleon's tongue may be twice the length of its body when stretched out to catch prey!

TOP 10

DON'T EAT ME!

Which reptiles are the best survival champions?

rattle

1 Keep away!

The rattlesnake shakes the "rattle" of empty scales on its tail to warn predators: "Keep away or I will bite you!"

2 Good-bye, tail!

Many lizards are able to snap off their tail when attacked. The tail distracts the predator long enough for the lizard to escape.

7 Prickly mouthful

To escape being eaten, the armadillo lizard holds its tail in its mouth and curls its sharp, spiny body into a prickly ball.

3 Frightening frill

The Australian frilled lizard scares predators or rivals by spreading its enormous neck frill. This makes it look big and dangerous.

8 Ace actors

Predators prefer to eat living prey. This Eastern hognose snake rolls over, pretending to be dead to put off hungry predators.

4 Hungry croc

Could you wait two years for a meal? A big crocodile can survive this long by using up fat stored in its tail and other body parts.

9 False head

The thorny devil has a false head behind its real one. It tucks its real head between its legs, so a predator attacks the wrong one!

5 Bloody eyes

If they are threatened, horned lizards sometimes squirt blood from their eyes! Most predators are so shocked, they think twice about attacking ...

10 Balloon body

When it's threatened, a puff adder swells up like a long balloon by taking air into its lungs. This makes it look twice as dangerous.

6 Stinky smell

The stinkpot turtle drives attackers away by squirting out a musky-smelling liquid from "stink glands" in the skin of its legs. What a stench!

Which survival champion is your number one?

THE REMARKABLE REPTILE QUIZ

Are you an expert on reptiles? Test your knowledge by completing this quiz! When you've answered all of the questions, turn to page 63 to check your score.

 Reptiles rely on their surroundings to warm up or cool down their body, meaning they are what?
a) Cold-blooded
b) Hot-blooded
c) Warm-blooded

 Scales are made out of the same substance as your hair. What is it called?
a) Dentine
b) Keratin
c) Plastic

 What are a tortoise's giant scales called?
a) Scutes
b) Solar scales
c) Super scales

 Which of the following is a type of lizard with no legs?
a) Sand worm
b) Slow worm
c) Smooth worm

 What do we call it when a snake sheds its old skin?
a) Scuffing
b) Shuffling
c) Sloughing

 Which of the following is a unique reptile that lives on islands off the coast of New Zealand?
a) Komodo dragon
b) Triceratops
c) Tuatara

 About how many species of snake are there?
a) 300
b) 3,000
c) 300,000

 Which reptile group do caimans belong to?
a) Crocodile family
b) Lizards
c) Snakes

Which type of lizard is the world's smallest reptile?
a) Chameleon
b) Gecko
c) Iguana

 What do leatherback turtles eat?
a) Flying fish
b) Jellyfish
c) Starfish

 Which sport do adders take part in when they compete for females?
a) Judo
b) Rugby
c) Wrestling

 Where do female turtles lay their eggs?
a) In coral caves
b) On the beach where they hatched
c) Under a pile of seaweed in the ocean

 Which reptile carries its hatchlings to water in its mouth?
a) Chameleon
b) Nile crocodile
c) Python

 Which kind of reptile are sidewinders?
a) Crocodiles
b) Lizards
c) Snakes

 Which lizard swims and feeds in the sea?
a) Marine boa
b) Marine chameleon
c) Marine iguana

 Which reptiles are the fastest on the planet?
a) Lizards
b) Turtles
c) Snakes

 Which lizard can run on water?
a) Basilisk lizard
b) Monitor lizard
c) Shapeshifter lizard

 Which kind of snake can fold back its fangs?
a) Cobra
b) Mamba
c) Viper

 What is the name of a lizard that looks like leaves on the rainforest floor?
a) Fern lizard
b) Kangaroo lizard
c) Litter lizard

 Which reptile cannot change its color?
a) Chameleon
b) Crocodile
c) Thorny devil

GLOSSARY

backbone
A flexible chain of bones in an animal's back, which supports the body. Animals with a backbone, such as reptiles, are called vertebrates.

bacteria
A large, varied group of very tiny, single-celled living things. Bacteria live in the soil, water, plants, and animals.

camouflage
Colors and patterns that help an animal to blend in with its surroundings.

clutch
A number of eggs that are all laid at the same time.

cold-blooded
Describes an animal whose body temperature varies with the temperature of its surroundings. Cold-blooded animals cannot control their own body temperature.

condense
When moisture in the air cools to become liquid, like steam from a kettle.

courtship
Behavior, such as bellowing, fighting, or showing off, that helps to decide which male and female will mate together.

dinosaurs
Prehistoric reptiles, such as Stegosaurus. Dinosaurs once ruled our planet, but died out 65 million years ago.

eardrum
A piece of thin skin in the ear that vibrates (shakes) when sound hits it. These vibrations turn into signals that travel to the brain so the animal "hears" the sound.

fangs
Long, pointed teeth, which may be used to deliver venom, especially in some snakes.

granular
Looking as if it is made of small, rounded grains, or crumbs.

hatchling
Any baby animal that emerges, or hatches, from an egg.

keratin
A horny substance that forms strong, flexible fibers and makes up part of a reptile's scales, as well as human fingernails and hair.

omnivore
An animal that eats a wide variety of food, both plants and animals.

oxygen
A gas in the air that living things need in order to release energy from their food.

predator
An animal that hunts and eats other animals for food.

prey
An animal that is killed and eaten by another animal.

pupil
The dark opening in the middle of the eye that allows light to enter.

rain forest
The warm, wet tropical forest that grows near the Equator (an imaginary line around the middle of the Earth).

rudder
A broad, flat piece of wood or metal joined to the back of a boat or an airplane. It is used for steering.

saliva
A colorless liquid produced in the mouth, which is also called "spit." It helps food to slide down the throat.

scutes
Large, horny scales that cover the shells of tortoises and turtles and the bodies of crocodiles.

skeleton
The bony framework that supports and protects an animal's body.

sloughing
Shedding old skin or scales from time to time. This process is also called molting.

species
A group of living things that share similar features and can breed together to produce fertile young.

streamlined
A smooth, slim shape that moves through air or water easily.

venom
A poisonous liquid that some reptiles (mainly snakes) use for hunting or self-defense.

QUIZ ANSWERS: 1 = a, 2 = b, 3 = a, 4 = b, 5 = c, 6 = c, 7 = b, 8 = a, 9 = a, 10 = b, 11 = c, 12 = b, 13 = b, 14 = c, 15 = c, 16 = a, 17 = a, 18 = c, 19 = b, 20 = b.

INDEX